# ANIMALS AT RISK
# CONDORS IN DANGER

BY N. D. HARASYMIW

Gareth Stevens
Publishing

Please visit our website, www.garethstevens.com. For a free color catalog of all our high-quality books, call toll free 1-800-542-2595 or fax 1-877-542-2596.

**Library of Congress Cataloging-in-Publication Data**

Harasymiw, N. D.
Condors in danger / by N.D. Harasymiw
pg. cm. — (Animals at risk)
Includes index.
ISBN 978-1-4339-9155-4 (pbk)
ISBN 978-1-4339-9156-1 (6-Pack)
ISBN 978-1-4339-9154-7 (library binding)
1.California condor — Juvenile literature. 2. Andean condor. 3. Endangered species — Juvenile literature. I. Title.
QL696.C53 H25 2014
598.92–dc23

First Edition

Published in 2014 by
**Gareth Stevens Publishing**
111 East 14th Street, Suite 349
New York, NY 10003

Copyright © 2014 Gareth Stevens Publishing

Designer: Andrea Davison-Bartolotta
Editor: Therese M. Shea

Photo credits: Cover, p. 1 James DeBoer/Shutterstock.com; pp. 4, 13 (both) David McNew/Getty Images; p. 5 (left) Ammit Jack/Shutterstock.com, (right) kojihirano/Shutterstock.com; p. 6 Eric Isselee/Shutterstock.com; p. 7 (main) Luis César Tejo/Shutterstock.com, (inset) Ferenc Cegledi/Shutterstock.com; p. 9 Mark Jones Roving Tortoise Photos/Oxford Scientific/Getty Images; p. 11 John Warburton-Lee/AWL Images/Getty Images; p. 12 Andy Dean Photography/Shutterstock.com; p. 14 Larry B. King/Shutterstock.com; p. 15 Kenneth W. Fink/Photo Researchers/Getty Images; p. 17 John Cancalosi/Peter Arnold/Getty Images; p. 18 Iakoc Filimonov/Shutterstock.com; p. 19 U.S. Fish and Wildlife Services via Wikimedia Commons; p. 20 Marilyn Angel Wynn/Nativestock/Getty Images.

Printed in the United States of America

CPSIA compliance information: Batch #CS13GS: For further information contact Gareth Stevens, New York, New York at 1-800-542-2595.

# CONTENTS

Words in the glossary appear in **bold** type the first time they are used in the text.

# BiRDS iN NEED

A condor is a kind of vulture. Condors eat mostly dead meat, or carrion, rather than live animals. Condors might sound like scary birds, but they need our help. They're in danger of becoming **extinct**!

There are only two kinds of condors. Both are found in the Americas. The California condor lives in California and Arizona. It's also found in Baja California, a part of Mexico. Andean condors live in the Andes Mountains of South America and along the coasts of Peru and Argentina.

## WILD FACTS
Vultures are birds of **prey**, which means they eat animals.

 The head of both Andean and California condors may change color when they're excited!

ANDEAN CONDOR

CALIFORNIA CONDOR

# Not-So-Pretty Birds

Both California and Andean condors have no feathers on their head and much of their neck. Their body is covered in black feathers.

There are ways to tell the birds apart. While both have feathers circling the base of their neck, this "collar" is black on California condors and white on Andean condors. Also, California condors have white feathers underneath their wings, and Andean condors have white feathers on the top of their wings. It's hard to call either condor cute!

ANDEAN CONDOR

Male Andean condors have a growth on their head.

MALE CALIFORNIA CONDOR

The Andean condor has one of the largest **wingspans** of any bird. Its wings may measure 10 feet (3 m) from tip to tip! The bird also weighs up to 33 pounds (15 kg). This makes it one of the largest flying birds in the world.

California condors are almost as large and heavy as Andean condors. In fact, they're the largest flying bird in North America.

Because they're so heavy, condors need some help to fly. They live in windy places so they can **glide** on strong air currents.

**WILD FACTS**

Both kinds of condors are often about 4 feet (1.2 m) tall.

▼ The Andean condor got its name from the Andes Mountains, one of its **habitats**.

# CRUISING FOR A MEAL

A condor's wingspan and air currents work very well together. The bird may only need to flap its wings once an hour! Condors fly long distances while keeping watch for a meal below. They can fly 2 miles (3.2 km) above the ground. It's a good thing condors have excellent eyesight!

Coastal areas provide the condor with carrion, such as dead seals and fish. Condors look for larger animals inland, such as cattle and deer. They may even grab eggs and baby birds from nests.

## WILD FACTS

Condors can eat so much they have to rest before taking flight again. They may not eat again for several days.

Eating carrion might sound gross, but condors help clean up the natural world by doing this!

# ON THE EDGE

By the late 1970s, fewer than 30 California condors were left in the world. Why were these high fliers in trouble? Many had been shot by hunters. Some died from eating poisoned animals meant to kill coyotes. Other condors died after eating the remains of animals that had been shot by **lead** bullets. This gave the birds lead poisoning.

The condors that remained faced other problems. People were building on land that had been condor habitats. The birds had less space to live and find food.

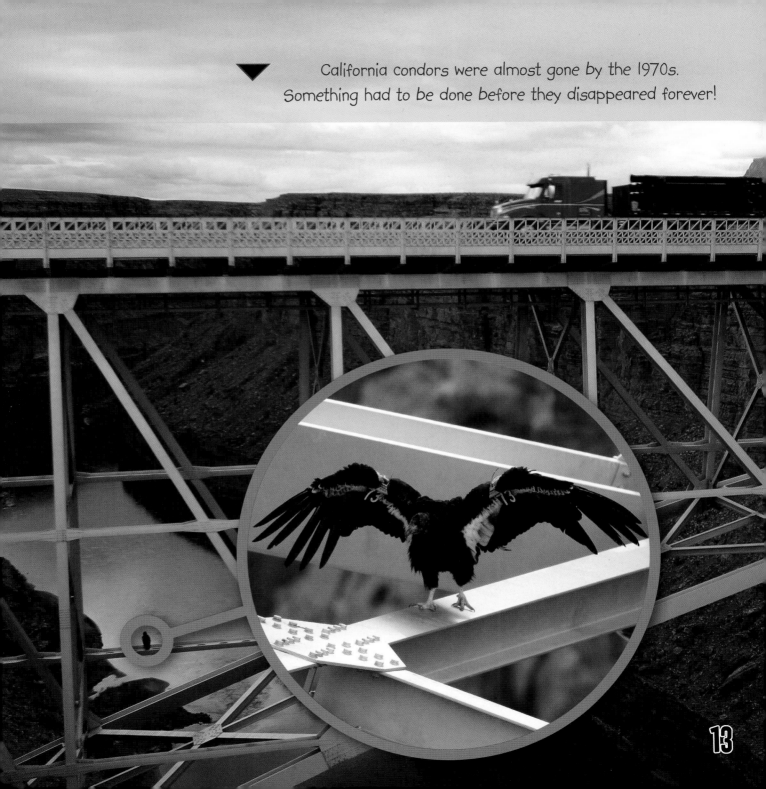

California condors were almost gone by the 1970s.
Something had to be done before they disappeared forever!

13

# LAST CHANCE

Between 1982 and 1987, scientists captured the remaining California condors. They raised the birds in **captivity**, safe from danger. In 1992, scientists began **releasing** some condors into the wild. Twenty years later, the condor population had grown from 22 to 200 condors!

Today, there are more than 400 California condors. Around 225 are in the wild. These condors still face some of the same problems that nearly killed their **species**. Scientists continue to keep watch on their numbers.

Condors in captivity may be tagged before they're released. This helps scientists keep track of them in the wild.

**WILD FACTS**
Condors make hissing and grunting sounds.

# MORE ACTION

The Andean condors were at risk, too. Many South Americans used the birds' bones and other body parts to make **medicines** for strength and health. On top of that, some killed condors to keep their livestock safe from attack. These people didn't know condors mostly eat carrion.

Andean condor numbers fell to a few thousand. Finally, a captivity plan began. Since 1990, more than 60 Andean condors have been raised in zoos and released into the wild of South America.

## WILD FACTS
The ancient Inca people of South America thought the condor brought the sun into the sky every morning.

Released birds can be tracked by **satellites** and radio waves. You can see a marker on this condor.

17

# DOUBLE CLUTCHING

One challenge of increasing the condor population is that condors don't have babies often. Female condors don't lay eggs until they're about 7 years old. Then they lay one egg every 2 years.

Scientists found that if an egg is removed, the mother will lay another. Scientists began collecting eggs from nests to make this happen. The method is called double clutching. The collected eggs are **incubated** until they're hatched. This way, a mother may have as many as two or even three babies every 2 years.

Condor chicks in the wild are cared for by both parents until they're about 1 year old. In zoos, chicks may be fed by a puppet—just like this one!

# THUNDERBIRDS

Though both condor captivity-and-release programs have been successful, the birds are still in danger. Their numbers aren't large enough to end the programs. Even now, they face dangers such as poisoning and power lines in their flight paths.

Native Americans called the condor the "thunderbird." They believed it made thunder with a flap of its wings. Though we know how thunder is made, a condor in flight does seem almost magical. Continuing to learn about and respect this amazing creature will help us keep it around for years to come.

THUNDERBIRD TOTEM POLE

# Operation Condor: Problem and Solutions

**Who:**

Condor Population

**Problem:**

**What:** People want to help the condor population grow.

**Why:** Condors are in danger of becoming extinct.

**Solutions:**

**Solution 1:**
Condors are captured and raised by scientists.

**Result:**
Condors are kept safe from man-made dangers.

**Solution 2:**
Double clutching helps condor mothers lay more eggs.

**Result:**
More condor babies are born more quickly.

# GLOSSARY

**captivity:** the state of being caged

**extinct:** no longer living

**glide:** to move in a smooth and graceful way

**habitat:** the natural place where an animal or plant lives

**incubate:** to keep eggs warm so they can hatch

**lead:** a bluish-gray matter used to make many objects such as bullets. Lead is poisonous if taken into the body.

**medicine:** a drug taken to make a sick person well

**prey:** an animal that is hunted by other animals for food

**release:** to set free

**satellite:** an object that circles Earth in order to collect and send information or aid in communication

**species:** a group of plants or animals that are all of the same kind

**wingspan:** the length between the tips of a pair of wings that are stretched out

# FOR MORE INFORMATION

## Books

Goldish, Meish. *California Condors: Saved by Captive Breeding*. New York, NY: Bearport Publishing, 2009.

Macken, JoAnn. *Condors*. Pleasantville, NY: Weekly Reader Publishing, 2010.

Silhol, Sandrine, and Gaëlle Guérive. *Extraordinary Endangered Animals*. New York, NY: Abrams Books for Young Readers, 2011.

## Websites

**Andean Condor**
*animals.nationalgeographic.com/animals/birds/andean-condor/*
Find out about the Andean condor and other kinds of birds.

**Birds: California Condor**
*www.sandiegozoo.org/animalbytes/t-condor.html*
Read many fun facts about these amazing big birds.

# INDEX